The Ukraine-Russia Conflict

Christoffer Smestad

Published by Christoffer Smestad, 2023.

THE UKRAINE-RUSSIA CONFLICT

First edition. April 16, 2023.

ISBN: 979-8223977292

Written by Christoffer Smestad.

Table of Contents

Chapter 1: Introduction 1

Chapter 2: The History of Ukraine and Russia 3

Chapter 3: Causes of the Conflict 5

Chapter 4: The Annexation of Crimea 7

Chapter 5: The Conflict in Eastern Ukraine 10

Chapter 6: The Humanitarian Crisis in Eastern Ukraine 12

Chapter 7: International Response to the Ukraine-Russia Conflict 16

Chapter 8: Human Rights Abuses in the Ukraine-Russia Conflict 18

Chapter 9: The Role of International Actors in the Ukraine-Russia Conflict 21

Chapter 10: The Human Cost of the Ukraine-Russia Conflict 25

Chapter 11: International Response to the Ukraine-Russia Conflict 29

Chapter 12: Humanitarian Impact 33

Chapter 13: Propaganda and Disinformation 36

Chapter 14: Military Technology and Strategy 39

Chapter 15: Humanitarian Crisis and Civilian Suffering 42

Chapter 16: Cyber Warfare 45

Chapter 17: International Response................................48

Chapter 18: Human Rights Violations 51

Chapter 19: Prospects for Peace 55

Chapter 20: Conclusion...59

Chapter 1: Introduction

The conflict between Ukraine and Russia is a complex and ongoing situation that has been ongoing since 2014. At its core, the conflict is about Ukraine's struggle for independence and Russia's attempts to maintain its sphere of influence in the region. The conflict has led to the deaths of thousands of people and displacement of millions.

The roots of the conflict can be traced back to the collapse of the Soviet Union in 1991. Following the dissolution of the Soviet Union, Ukraine became an independent state and developed close ties with Russia. However, tensions began to emerge over time, with Ukraine seeking to assert its independence and Russia seeking to maintain its influence in the region.

The conflict escalated in 2013 when protests broke out in Ukraine over the country's decision to back out of a deal with the European Union in favor of closer ties with Russia. This led to the ousting of Ukrainian President Viktor Yanukovych in 2014 and Russia's subsequent annexation of Crimea.

Since then, the conflict has centered on the separatist movements in eastern Ukraine, which are believed to have been backed by Russia. Despite ongoing diplomatic efforts to resolve the situation, the conflict remains unresolved, with sporadic fighting and violations of the ceasefire.

This book aims to provide an in-depth analysis of the conflict, examining its causes, key players, and ongoing impact on Ukraine and Russia. It will explore the various political, economic, and social factors that have contributed to the conflict, as well as the role of propaganda, disinformation, and military technology. By examining the conflict from a range of perspectives, this book will provide readers with a comprehensive understanding of the ongoing situation in Ukraine and its broader implications for the region and the world.

Chapter 2: The History of Ukraine and Russia

To understand the conflict between Ukraine and Russia, it is important to examine the historical relationship between the two countries. Ukraine has been part of the Russian Empire, the Soviet Union, and an independent state. Over time, the relationship between Ukraine and Russia has been characterized by both cooperation and tension.

During the Russian Empire, Ukraine was a region under Russian control. However, in the aftermath of the Bolshevik Revolution in 1917, Ukraine declared its independence and formed the Ukrainian People's Republic. The republic did not last long, however, as it was quickly overtaken by Soviet forces and became part of the Soviet Union.

Under Soviet rule, Ukraine was an important industrial and agricultural region, and its economy grew rapidly. However, Ukrainian identity and language were suppressed, and many Ukrainians were killed or imprisoned during Stalin's purges in the 1930s.

Ukrainian independence was restored in 1991 following the collapse of the Soviet Union. However, many Ukrainians continued to feel a strong connection to Russia, and the two countries maintained close economic and political ties.

Despite this, tensions began to emerge between Ukraine and Russia over time, particularly with regards to Ukraine's desire for greater independence and its efforts to align with the West. These tensions eventually led to the conflict that erupted in 2014.

Today, Ukraine and Russia continue to have a complex and fraught relationship. While the conflict has brought relations between the two countries to a new low, there are still deep ties between them, including economic, cultural, and historical connections. Understanding this history is crucial to understanding the ongoing conflict and its potential future trajectory.

Chapter 3: Causes of the Conflict

The conflict between Ukraine and Russia has complex and multifaceted causes, including political, economic, and historical factors. In this chapter, we will examine some of the key causes of the conflict.

One major factor is Ukraine's desire for greater independence and closer ties with the West. This desire was fueled by a sense that Ukraine's economic and political potential was being limited by its close ties to Russia. When Ukrainian President Viktor Yanukovych backed out of a deal with the European Union in favor of closer ties with Russia, it sparked protests and ultimately led to Yanukovych's ousting.

Another factor is Russia's desire to maintain its sphere of influence in the region. Russia sees Ukraine as a crucial buffer zone between itself and NATO, and views any attempt by Ukraine to align with the West as a threat to its national security. Russia also has a significant population of ethnic Russians living in Ukraine, particularly in the Crimea region.

Propaganda and disinformation have also played a significant role in fueling the conflict. Both Russia and Ukraine have used media outlets to promote their own narratives and demonize the other side. This has led to a high level of mistrust and hostility between the two countries, and has made it difficult to reach a resolution to the conflict.

Military technology has also played a significant role in the conflict. Russia has provided support to separatist groups in eastern Ukraine, including weapons and training. This has enabled the separatists to gain control of a significant portion of the region, and has led to ongoing clashes with Ukrainian government forces.

Finally, corruption and political instability in Ukraine have also contributed to the conflict. Corruption is widespread in Ukraine, and many Ukrainians feel that their government is not doing enough to address the country's economic and social problems. This has fueled resentment and a sense of alienation among many Ukrainians, and has made it difficult for the government to maintain control over the country.

Overall, the conflict between Ukraine and Russia is a complex and multifaceted issue with deep roots in history, politics, economics, and culture. Understanding the various causes of the conflict is crucial to finding a resolution and preventing further escalation of the conflict.

Chapter 4: The Annexation of Crimea

One of the major events that sparked the current conflict between Ukraine and Russia was the annexation of Crimea in March 2014. In this chapter, we will explore the circumstances surrounding the annexation and its impact on the conflict.

Crimea is a peninsula in the Black Sea that was historically part of Russia. However, in 1954, Soviet leader Nikita Khrushchev transferred control of Crimea to Ukraine as a symbolic gesture of friendship between the two countries. When Ukraine gained independence in 1991, Crimea remained part of the country, but many of its residents identified more strongly with Russia than with Ukraine.

In 2014, protests erupted in Ukraine against the pro-Russian government of President Viktor Yanukovych. Yanukovych fled the country, and a new government was formed, which was more aligned with the West. This change in government was seen as a threat to Russia's interests in the region, particularly given the large population of ethnic Russians in Ukraine.

In response, Russian forces, without official insignia and believed to be Russian special forces, seized control of key government buildings and military bases in Crimea. A referendum was held, which was widely criticized as illegitimate by Western countries, in which a majority of Crimeans voted to join Russia. Russia subsequently annexed Crimea, which was met with condemnation from the international community.

The annexation of Crimea had significant implications for the conflict between Ukraine and Russia. It further escalated tensions between the two countries and led to ongoing clashes in eastern Ukraine between Ukrainian government forces and separatist groups backed by Russia. The annexation also sparked international sanctions against Russia, which have had a significant impact on the country's economy.

Overall, the annexation of Crimea was a key moment in the conflict between Ukraine and Russia, and it continues to be a major source of tension between the two countries.

Following the annexation of Crimea, Russia took steps to solidify its control over the territory. It deployed troops, set up border checkpoints, and established a new government in the region. The Russian authorities also began to crack down on any signs of dissent or opposition to the annexation.

Crimea's status as part of Russia is not recognized by the majority of countries in the world, including the United States and the European Union. In response to the annexation, the international community imposed a range of economic and political sanctions on Russia. These sanctions targeted Russian individuals and businesses, as well as sectors of the Russian economy, such as finance, energy, and defense.

The annexation of Crimea also had significant humanitarian implications. Many Crimean Tatars, an ethnic group that was deported from Crimea by Soviet authorities in the 1940s, expressed concerns about their safety and security under Russian rule. The Tatars have faced discrimination and persecution in the past, and many fear a return to the abuses they suffered under Soviet rule.

In addition, the annexation has had a significant impact on the Ukrainian economy. Crimea was an important tourist destination, and its loss has had a negative impact on Ukraine's tourism industry. It has also had implications for Ukraine's energy security, as Russia's annexation of Crimea gave it control over key energy infrastructure in the region.

Overall, the annexation of Crimea has had significant and far-reaching implications for the conflict between Ukraine and Russia. It has further escalated tensions between the two countries, led to ongoing clashes in eastern Ukraine, and had significant humanitarian and economic consequences. The annexation remains a major point of contention between Ukraine and Russia, and it is unlikely to be resolved any time soon.

Chapter 5: The Conflict in Eastern Ukraine

Following the annexation of Crimea, tensions between Ukraine and Russia continued to escalate, and the conflict spread to eastern Ukraine. In this chapter, we will explore the origins of the conflict in eastern Ukraine, its key players, and its impact on the region.

The conflict in eastern Ukraine began in the spring of 2014 when separatist groups in the Donetsk and Luhansk regions, with support from Russia, declared independence from Ukraine. The separatists established their own governments and began to take control of territory in the region, including key cities such as Donetsk and Luhansk.

The Ukrainian government responded with a military crackdown on the separatists, which led to a protracted and bloody conflict. The conflict has been characterized by intense fighting, shelling, and artillery fire, and has resulted in thousands of deaths and displacement of civilians.

The conflict has also involved a range of actors, including Ukrainian government forces, separatist groups, Russian military personnel, and volunteer fighters from both Ukraine and Russia. The conflict has been fueled by Russia's support for the separatists, which has included the provision of weapons, training, and personnel.

The conflict has had a significant impact on the region. The fighting has damaged infrastructure, including schools, hospitals, and housing, and has led to a humanitarian crisis. Many civilians have been forced to flee their homes, and those who remain are often without access to basic services such as electricity, water, and healthcare.

The conflict has also had wider implications for Ukraine and the region. It has strained Ukraine's relationship with Russia and its ties with the West. The conflict has also had implications for European security, as it has raised concerns about Russian aggression and expansionism.

Efforts to resolve the conflict have been ongoing, but have thus far been unsuccessful. The Minsk agreements, signed in 2015, were intended to provide a framework for a peaceful resolution to the conflict, but fighting has continued, and the situation remains volatile.

Overall, the conflict in eastern Ukraine has had significant and far-reaching implications for the region and beyond. It has resulted in a protracted and bloody conflict, a humanitarian crisis, and strained relations between Ukraine, Russia, and the West. Resolving the conflict remains a significant challenge, and its impact is likely to be felt for years to come.

Chapter 6: The Humanitarian Crisis in Eastern Ukraine

The ongoing conflict in eastern Ukraine has had a devastating impact on the region's civilian population, resulting in a severe humanitarian crisis. In this chapter, we will explore the scope of the crisis, the challenges facing aid organizations, and the impact on the lives of civilians.

The conflict has resulted in the displacement of over 1.5 million people, with many forced to flee their homes due to the fighting. Those who remain in the conflict-affected areas often live in precarious conditions, with limited access to basic necessities such as food, water, and medical care.

The conflict has also had a significant impact on the region's infrastructure. Schools, hospitals, and other critical infrastructure have been damaged or destroyed, further exacerbating the humanitarian situation.

Aid organizations have struggled to respond to the crisis, facing significant challenges in accessing conflict-affected areas and providing assistance to those in need. The conflict has also made it difficult to coordinate relief efforts, with the different parties to the conflict often imposing restrictions on aid organizations' activities.

The humanitarian crisis has had a significant impact on the lives of civilians in the region. Many face a daily struggle to access basic necessities, and the psychological toll of the conflict has been significant, particularly for children. The conflict has also resulted in a rise in gender-based violence and human trafficking, further exacerbating the crisis.

The international community has responded to the crisis with a range of measures, including providing humanitarian aid, imposing sanctions on Russia, and supporting peace talks. However, more needs to be done to address the humanitarian crisis and provide assistance to those in need.

Overall, the humanitarian crisis in eastern Ukraine is a tragic consequence of the ongoing conflict. The conflict has had a devastating impact on the lives of civilians, and addressing the crisis requires a sustained and coordinated international effort.

Despite the challenges facing aid organizations, there have been significant efforts to provide assistance to those affected by the conflict. The United Nations and other international organizations have provided humanitarian aid, including food, water, and medical supplies. Non-governmental organizations (NGOs) and local organizations have also played a critical role in providing assistance to those in need.

In addition to providing immediate relief, aid organizations have also worked to address the long-term impacts of the conflict on the region's population. This has included efforts to address the psychological trauma experienced by civilians, as well as support for economic recovery and reconstruction.

However, the ongoing conflict and restrictions on access to conflict-affected areas continue to pose significant challenges to relief efforts. Aid organizations have called for increased access to conflict-affected areas and for parties to the conflict to respect international humanitarian law.

The impact of the humanitarian crisis on children has been particularly significant. Many children have been forced to flee their homes, resulting in disrupted education and psychological trauma. The conflict has also resulted in a rise in child labor and exploitation, including recruitment by armed groups.

Efforts have been made to address the needs of children affected by the conflict. UNICEF and other organizations have provided support for education and psychological counseling, as well as protection from exploitation and recruitment by armed groups.

The impact of the conflict on women has also been significant, with reports of gender-based violence and sexual exploitation. The conflict has also resulted in a rise in the number of female-headed households, which are often more vulnerable to poverty and displacement.

Efforts to address the needs of women affected by the conflict have included support for gender-based violence prevention and response, as well as efforts to promote women's participation in peacebuilding and conflict resolution.

Overall, the humanitarian crisis in eastern Ukraine remains a significant challenge, and addressing the needs of those affected by the conflict will require sustained and coordinated efforts. Despite the challenges facing relief efforts, aid organizations and local communities continue to work tirelessly to provide assistance to those in need, and their efforts are crucial in mitigating the impact of the crisis on the region's civilian population.

Chapter 7: International Response to the Ukraine-Russia Conflict

The Ukraine-Russia conflict has been a significant challenge for the international community, with tensions between the two countries affecting global politics and security. In this chapter, we will explore the international response to the conflict, including diplomatic efforts, economic sanctions, and military aid.

Diplomatic efforts have played a significant role in attempts to resolve the conflict. The Minsk II agreement, signed in 2015, outlined a ceasefire and a roadmap for a political solution to the conflict. The agreement was brokered by France and Germany, and while it has not led to a complete resolution of the conflict, it has helped to reduce the intensity of fighting in the region.

The United Nations has also played a role in the conflict, with the Security Council passing multiple resolutions calling for an end to the violence and the protection of civilians. However, disagreements among the Security Council's permanent members have limited the effectiveness of these resolutions.

Economic sanctions have been a key tool used by the international community to pressure Russia to de-escalate the conflict. The European Union and the United States have imposed a range of sanctions, including restrictions on trade, travel, and access to financial markets. These sanctions have had a significant impact on the Russian economy, with some estimates suggesting that they have cost the country billions of dollars in lost trade and investment.

Military aid has also been provided to Ukraine by several countries, including the United States, Canada, and the United Kingdom. This aid has included weapons, training, and other support, aimed at helping Ukraine defend itself against Russian aggression. However, concerns have been raised about the potential for military aid to escalate the conflict and lead to further violence.

Efforts to resolve the conflict through diplomatic means have faced significant challenges, with deep-rooted tensions between Ukraine and Russia and disagreements among the international community on how best to address the conflict. Economic sanctions have had a significant impact on Russia but have not led to a complete resolution of the conflict. Military aid has helped Ukraine defend itself but also carries the risk of escalating the violence.

Overall, the international response to the Ukraine-Russia conflict has been complex and multifaceted, with no easy solutions. However, diplomatic efforts, economic sanctions, and military aid remain important tools in efforts to de-escalate the conflict and bring about a lasting peace.

Chapter 8: Human Rights Abuses in the Ukraine-Russia Conflict

The Ukraine-Russia conflict has been characterized by a range of human rights abuses, including violence against civilians, torture, and enforced disappearances. In this chapter, we will explore some of the human rights abuses that have been reported in the context of the conflict.

Violence against civilians has been a significant concern throughout the conflict, with reports of indiscriminate shelling and bombing of residential areas, resulting in the deaths of civilians, including women and children. Both sides have been accused of using heavy weapons in densely populated areas, resulting in significant civilian casualties.

Torture has also been reported in the conflict, with both Ukrainian and Russian-backed separatist forces accused of using torture and other forms of ill-treatment against detainees. Detainees have reported being subjected to beatings, electric shocks, and other forms of physical and psychological abuse.

Enforced disappearances have also been reported in the conflict, with individuals being detained and held incommunicado by both sides. Families of those who have disappeared have reported difficulties in obtaining information about the whereabouts of their loved ones and in gaining access to legal remedies.

In addition to these abuses, there have also been reports of restrictions on freedom of expression, freedom of assembly, and freedom of the press. Journalists and activists have been targeted for their reporting on the conflict, with some facing threats, harassment, and even imprisonment.

The international community has condemned these human rights abuses and called for those responsible to be held accountable. The United Nations has called for an end to the violence and for parties to the conflict to respect international human rights and humanitarian law. Human rights organizations have also documented abuses and advocated for accountability.

Despite these efforts, the human rights situation in the conflict-affected areas remains challenging, with ongoing reports of abuses and limited access to justice for victims. Addressing human rights abuses in the context of the conflict will require sustained efforts by both the international community and parties to the conflict to uphold human rights and ensure accountability for abuses.

Efforts to address human rights abuses in the context of the Ukraine-Russia conflict have faced significant challenges. The conflict has been marked by intense fighting and a breakdown in the rule of law, making it difficult to investigate and prosecute abuses. The political tensions between Ukraine and Russia have also complicated efforts to address human rights concerns, with each side blaming the other for the abuses that have been reported.

Human rights organizations and international bodies have played a critical role in documenting human rights abuses and advocating for accountability. Organizations such as Amnesty International and Human Rights Watch have published reports detailing abuses committed by both sides and calling for those responsible to be held accountable.

International bodies such as the United Nations have also been actively involved in efforts to address human rights abuses in the conflict. The United Nations Human Rights Monitoring Mission in Ukraine (HRMMU) has been documenting human rights violations in the country since 2014. The HRMMU has documented a range of abuses, including extrajudicial killings, enforced disappearances, and torture, and has called for those responsible to be held accountable.

Despite these efforts, impunity for human rights abuses remains a significant concern. In many cases, those responsible for abuses have not been held accountable, and victims have not received justice. The lack of accountability for human rights abuses can contribute to a cycle of violence and further abuses.

Addressing human rights abuses in the context of the Ukraine-Russia conflict will require sustained efforts by both parties to the conflict, as well as the international community. Efforts to ensure accountability for abuses and to uphold human rights will be critical in building a lasting peace in the region.

Chapter 9: The Role of International Actors in the Ukraine-Russia Conflict

The Ukraine-Russia conflict has not been confined to the borders of the two countries, with international actors playing a significant role in the conflict. In this chapter, we will explore the role of international actors in the conflict and their efforts to address the ongoing crisis.

The conflict has been the subject of significant international attention since its outbreak in 2014. The United States, European Union, and other Western countries have condemned Russia's annexation of Crimea and have imposed sanctions against Russia in response. The international community has also expressed concern about the ongoing violence in the Donbas region and has called for a peaceful resolution to the conflict.

The United Nations has played a key role in efforts to address the conflict, with the Security Council passing a series of resolutions aimed at ending the violence and protecting civilians. The UN has also established a mission to monitor the human rights situation in Ukraine and has called for an end to the violence and respect for human rights and international humanitarian law.

In addition to diplomatic efforts, international actors have also provided significant economic and military support to Ukraine. The United States has provided Ukraine with military aid and training, while the European Union has provided economic and technical assistance to support Ukraine's reforms and economic recovery. NATO has also increased its presence in the region, conducting military exercises and providing support to Ukraine.

Russia, for its part, has accused the West of interfering in the conflict and has denied any involvement in the violence in Ukraine. Russia has also sought support from other countries, particularly in the former Soviet bloc, and has criticized Western sanctions and support for Ukraine.

The role of international actors in the conflict remains complex and controversial, with different countries and organizations pursuing different strategies and objectives. While the international community has been united in its condemnation of Russia's annexation of Crimea, there are differences of opinion about how best to address the ongoing conflict in the Donbas region.

Efforts to address the conflict will require continued engagement and coordination among international actors. The involvement of the United States, European Union, and other Western countries will be critical in supporting Ukraine's stability and promoting a peaceful resolution to the conflict. At the same time, it will be important to engage with Russia and seek a constructive dialogue to address the underlying political and economic issues driving the conflict.

International efforts to address the Ukraine-Russia conflict have faced significant challenges, with the conflict continuing to escalate in some areas despite diplomatic efforts. The conflict has also highlighted the limits of international law and institutions in resolving complex conflicts and addressing human rights abuses.

One major challenge has been the lack of a clear path to resolving the conflict. While international actors have called for a peaceful resolution to the conflict, there is little agreement on how to achieve this goal. Some have advocated for negotiations between Ukraine and Russia, while others have called for greater pressure on Russia to withdraw its military forces from Ukraine.

Another challenge has been the complexity of the conflict, with multiple actors involved and competing interests at play. The conflict has not only pitted Ukraine against Russia, but has also involved pro-Russian separatists in eastern Ukraine and various international actors with different interests and objectives.

The conflict has also highlighted the limits of international law and institutions in addressing human rights abuses in the context of a conflict. While international actors have called for accountability for human rights abuses, the political complexities of the conflict have made it difficult to achieve justice for victims.

Despite these challenges, international actors continue to play a critical role in efforts to address the Ukraine-Russia conflict. Ongoing diplomatic efforts and economic support for Ukraine have helped to maintain international pressure on Russia and support Ukraine's stability. Human rights organizations and international bodies continue to document and raise awareness of human rights abuses in the conflict, calling for accountability for those responsible.

The role of international actors in the conflict is likely to continue to evolve in the coming years, as the conflict continues and new challenges emerge. The ongoing conflict in Ukraine highlights the importance of international cooperation and the need for a coordinated, sustained effort to address complex conflicts and promote peace and stability.

Chapter 10: The Human Cost of the Ukraine-Russia Conflict

The Ukraine-Russia conflict has had a devastating impact on the people of Ukraine, with tens of thousands killed and millions displaced from their homes. In this chapter, we will examine the human cost of the conflict and the ongoing humanitarian crisis in Ukraine.

Since the conflict began in 2014, thousands of people have been killed in fighting in eastern Ukraine, including Ukrainian soldiers, pro-Russian separatists, and civilians caught in the crossfire. The conflict has also resulted in significant damage to infrastructure and the economy, exacerbating the humanitarian crisis.

The conflict has forced millions of Ukrainians to flee their homes, with many seeking refuge in other parts of Ukraine or in neighboring countries. As of 2021, an estimated 1.5 million people remained displaced within Ukraine, while more than 1 million had fled to neighboring countries, such as Russia, Belarus, and Poland.

The humanitarian crisis has been exacerbated by ongoing violence, with civilians often caught in the crossfire between Ukrainian forces and pro-Russian separatists. Human rights organizations have documented widespread human rights abuses, including unlawful detention, torture, and extrajudicial killings by both sides of the conflict.

The ongoing conflict has also had a significant impact on the healthcare system in Ukraine, with hospitals and clinics damaged or destroyed by the conflict. This has left many Ukrainians without access to vital healthcare services, particularly in the conflict-affected regions.

International humanitarian organizations have been working to provide assistance to those affected by the conflict, including food, shelter, and medical care. However, ongoing violence and access restrictions have made it difficult to reach those in need, particularly in the conflict-affected areas.

The human cost of the Ukraine-Russia conflict has been significant, with millions of people affected by the ongoing violence and humanitarian crisis. The conflict has highlighted the importance of protecting civilians in the context of armed conflict and the urgent need for a peaceful resolution to the conflict to prevent further suffering.

Efforts to address the humanitarian crisis will require continued international support, including funding for humanitarian assistance and efforts to protect civilians from ongoing violence. It will also be important to ensure accountability for human rights abuses committed during the conflict and to support the rehabilitation and reintegration of those affected by the conflict.

The humanitarian crisis in Ukraine has been further compounded by the COVID-19 pandemic, which has added new challenges to the already difficult situation. The pandemic has disrupted supply chains and limited access to essential medical supplies, exacerbating existing health challenges and leaving many vulnerable populations at risk.

The pandemic has also had a significant impact on the economy, particularly in the conflict-affected regions. The closure of businesses and the disruption of trade have resulted in widespread unemployment and economic insecurity, making it even more difficult for people to access basic necessities.

The ongoing humanitarian crisis in Ukraine highlights the need for increased attention and support for vulnerable populations affected by the conflict. It also underscores the importance of ensuring that humanitarian aid reaches those who need it most, particularly in the conflict-affected areas where access to basic services has been severely limited.

International actors have an important role to play in addressing the humanitarian crisis in Ukraine, including providing financial support for humanitarian efforts and advocating for a peaceful resolution to the conflict. International organizations, such as the United Nations and the International Committee of the Red Cross, have been working to provide assistance to those affected by the conflict, but ongoing violence and access restrictions have made it difficult to reach those in need.

In addition to addressing the immediate humanitarian needs of those affected by the conflict, it will also be important to support longer-term efforts to rebuild infrastructure and promote economic development in the conflict-affected regions. This will require sustained international support and a commitment to addressing the root causes of the conflict.

In conclusion, the ongoing humanitarian crisis in Ukraine is a stark reminder of the human cost of conflict and the urgent need for a peaceful resolution to the Ukraine-Russia conflict. International actors must continue to provide support to those affected by the conflict and work towards a peaceful resolution to prevent further suffering and promote stability and prosperity in the region.

Chapter 11: International Response to the Ukraine-Russia Conflict

The Ukraine-Russia conflict has been the subject of international concern and has led to a number of diplomatic efforts to resolve the conflict peacefully. In this chapter, we will examine the international response to the conflict and the efforts to achieve a peaceful resolution.

From the outset, the international community has been closely monitoring the situation in Ukraine and has condemned Russia's annexation of Crimea and support for separatist rebels in eastern Ukraine. The United Nations, the European Union, and other regional organizations have taken a number of steps to address the conflict, including imposing economic sanctions and supporting diplomatic efforts to resolve the conflict.

The United Nations has played an important role in the international response to the conflict, with the UN Security Council issuing a number of resolutions calling for a peaceful resolution to the conflict and the protection of civilians. The UN has also supported efforts to provide humanitarian assistance to those affected by the conflict, and has worked to promote human rights and the rule of law in Ukraine.

The European Union has also been active in responding to the conflict, imposing economic sanctions on Russia and supporting diplomatic efforts to resolve the conflict. The EU has also provided significant financial assistance to Ukraine to support economic and social development, as well as humanitarian assistance to those affected by the conflict.

Other regional organizations, such as the Organization for Security and Cooperation in Europe (OSCE), have also been involved in efforts to address the conflict. The OSCE has played a key role in monitoring the ceasefire and supporting diplomatic efforts to resolve the conflict through the Minsk agreements.

Despite these efforts, the conflict has remained unresolved, with sporadic fighting and ongoing tensions between Ukraine and Russia. The international community continues to call for a peaceful resolution to the conflict, and diplomatic efforts to resolve the conflict have been ongoing.

In 2021, the United States and the European Union imposed new sanctions on Russia in response to the ongoing conflict and human rights abuses committed in Crimea and eastern Ukraine. The international community has also continued to provide support for humanitarian assistance to those affected by the conflict, and has called for increased efforts to address the root causes of the conflict and promote stability and development in the region.

In conclusion, the international response to the Ukraine-Russia conflict has been multifaceted, with a range of diplomatic, economic, and humanitarian measures aimed at resolving the conflict and addressing the humanitarian crisis. While progress has been made, the conflict remains unresolved, highlighting the need for continued international attention and support to achieve a peaceful resolution and promote stability and development in Ukraine and the wider region.

Efforts to resolve the Ukraine-Russia conflict through diplomatic means have continued, despite the challenges and obstacles that have been faced. One of the key diplomatic initiatives has been the Minsk agreements, which were signed in 2015 and aimed to achieve a ceasefire and a political resolution to the conflict.

The Minsk agreements were negotiated with the support of the OSCE, and involved representatives from Ukraine, Russia, and the separatist rebels in eastern Ukraine. The agreements called for a ceasefire, the withdrawal of heavy weapons from the conflict zone, and the establishment of a special status for the Donbas region in eastern Ukraine.

While the Minsk agreements were seen as a positive step towards a peaceful resolution to the conflict, they have faced significant challenges in implementation. Ceasefires have been repeatedly violated, and progress towards the political elements of the agreements has been slow. Nonetheless, the Minsk agreements remain the basis for diplomatic efforts to resolve the conflict, and the international community continues to support their implementation.

Other diplomatic initiatives have also been pursued, including efforts to promote dialogue and negotiations between Ukraine and Russia. The Normandy Format, which involves the leaders of Ukraine, Russia, Germany, and France, has been used to facilitate discussions on the conflict and support the implementation of the Minsk agreements. In addition, the Trilateral Contact Group, which includes representatives from Ukraine, Russia, and the OSCE, has been established to support the implementation of the ceasefire and other elements of the Minsk agreements.

Despite these diplomatic efforts, the conflict remains unresolved and tensions between Ukraine and Russia continue to simmer. The ongoing conflict in eastern Ukraine, the annexation of Crimea, and the broader geopolitical tensions between Russia and the West have contributed to a complex and challenging situation.

The international community has called for continued diplomatic efforts to resolve the conflict and promote stability in the region. In addition to diplomatic initiatives, efforts to support economic and social development in Ukraine and the wider region are seen as crucial to addressing the root causes of the conflict and promoting long-term stability.

Overall, the international response to the Ukraine-Russia conflict highlights the challenges of resolving complex geopolitical conflicts through diplomatic means. While progress has been made, much remains to be done to achieve a peaceful resolution to the conflict and promote stability and development in Ukraine and the wider region.

Chapter 12: Humanitarian Impact

The conflict between Ukraine and Russia has had significant humanitarian consequences, with millions of people affected by the violence and displacement. According to the United Nations, the conflict has resulted in over 13,000 deaths and more than 1.5 million people displaced within Ukraine, while over 1 million people have fled to neighbouring countries.

The humanitarian situation in eastern Ukraine remains a concern, with many people struggling to access basic necessities such as food, water, and healthcare. The ongoing conflict has also had a significant impact on the region's economy, with many businesses and industries disrupted by the violence and instability.

The displacement of millions of people has also put a strain on the resources of neighbouring countries, with many refugees facing challenges accessing basic services and support. While international aid has helped to alleviate some of the humanitarian impacts of the conflict, much more support is needed to address the ongoing needs of those affected by the violence.

In addition to the immediate humanitarian consequences of the conflict, there are also long-term impacts to consider. The ongoing violence and instability have disrupted social and economic development in the region, with consequences that could be felt for years to come.

There are also concerns about the impact of the conflict on regional stability and security. The annexation of Crimea and the ongoing conflict in eastern Ukraine have contributed to a broader geopolitical tension between Russia and the West, which has implications for regional and global security.

The international community has responded to the humanitarian crisis in various ways, including providing aid to those affected by the conflict and supporting efforts to address the root causes of the conflict. However, the ongoing violence and instability in the region continue to pose significant humanitarian challenges, and much more needs to be done to address the needs of those affected by the conflict and promote long-term stability in the region.

One of the key challenges in addressing the humanitarian crisis in Ukraine is the ongoing conflict itself. The violence and instability have made it difficult to deliver aid and support to those in need, and many aid organizations have faced challenges accessing conflict-affected areas.

In addition, there are also logistical challenges to providing humanitarian assistance in Ukraine, such as the need to transport aid through checkpoints and borders that may be closed or heavily regulated. This has made it difficult to provide timely and effective aid to those who need it most.

Another challenge is the limited funding for humanitarian assistance in Ukraine. While there have been some significant pledges of support from the international community, the ongoing conflict and competing humanitarian crises around the world have meant that there is a limited amount of funding available for Ukraine.

There are also challenges related to coordination and cooperation between different humanitarian organizations and actors. In order to provide effective assistance to those affected by the conflict, it is essential that aid organizations and other actors work together in a coordinated and strategic manner.

Despite these challenges, there have been some significant efforts to address the humanitarian crisis in Ukraine. The United Nations has launched various initiatives to provide aid and support to those affected by the conflict, and many other organizations and actors have also provided assistance.

Efforts have also been made to address some of the root causes of the conflict and promote long-term stability in the region. This includes supporting initiatives for political dialogue and peace negotiations, as well as promoting social and economic development in conflict-affected areas.

However, much more needs to be done to address the ongoing humanitarian crisis in Ukraine. This will require sustained and coordinated efforts from the international community, as well as continued engagement and support from Ukrainian authorities and other local actors.

Chapter 13: Propaganda and Disinformation

The conflict between Ukraine and Russia has also had significant implications for the global political landscape, particularly in relation to the relationship between Russia and the West.

The annexation of Crimea in 2014 was a major event that caused widespread concern and condemnation from the international community. Many Western countries responded with economic sanctions and other measures against Russia, while Russia has responded with its own sanctions and counter-measures.

The conflict in eastern Ukraine has also contributed to tensions between Russia and the West, with both sides accusing the other of contributing to the conflict and exacerbating tensions in the region. The ongoing conflict has also led to a broader geopolitical tension between Russia and the West, with implications for regional and global security.

The conflict has also highlighted the challenges and complexities of the post-Cold War global order. The principles of sovereignty, territorial integrity, and respect for international law have been called into question, with both sides accusing the other of violating these principles.

The crisis in Ukraine has also led to renewed discussions about the role of international organizations such as the United

Nations and the Organization for Security and Cooperation in Europe (OSCE) in promoting peace and stability in the region. The conflict has highlighted the need for more effective mechanisms for conflict resolution and prevention, as well as greater cooperation and dialogue between international actors.

The crisis in Ukraine has also had implications for the global economy, particularly in relation to energy markets. Ukraine is an important transit country for Russian gas exports to Europe, and the conflict has led to concerns about the security and stability of energy supplies.

Overall, the crisis in Ukraine has had significant implications for the global political and economic landscape. It has highlighted the challenges of promoting peace and stability in a rapidly changing and increasingly interconnected world, and has underlined the importance of cooperation and dialogue between international actors in addressing these challenges.

The crisis in Ukraine has also had implications for the global security landscape. The conflict has led to a renewed focus on military readiness and defense spending in many countries, particularly in Europe.

NATO has responded to the crisis by increasing its military presence in the region and conducting military exercises. This has led to concerns from Russia about the expansion of NATO and the potential for further escalation of tensions.

The conflict has also led to concerns about the proliferation of weapons, particularly in relation to the illegal trade in small arms and light weapons. The conflict has highlighted the need for greater efforts to control and regulate the trade in arms and to prevent the flow of weapons to conflict-affected areas.

The humanitarian crisis in Ukraine has also had implications for global migration patterns. The conflict has led to the displacement of millions of people, both within Ukraine and across borders. This has contributed to the ongoing refugee crisis in Europe and has placed a significant burden on neighboring countries such as Poland and Turkey.

The crisis in Ukraine has also had implications for international law, particularly in relation to the principles of territorial integrity and sovereignty. The annexation of Crimea by Russia has been widely condemned as a violation of international law, and the ongoing conflict in eastern Ukraine has led to further concerns about the respect for these principles.

Overall, the crisis in Ukraine has had significant and far-reaching implications for the global political, economic, and security landscape. It has highlighted the complex and interrelated nature of modern conflicts, and the importance of international cooperation and dialogue in promoting peace and stability in the world.

Chapter 14: Military Technology and Strategy

The conflict in Ukraine has also showcased the use of modern military technology and strategies by both sides.

Russia has made use of its advanced military technology, including unmanned aerial vehicles (UAVs) and sophisticated anti-aircraft systems, to gain an advantage over Ukrainian forces. These technologies have enabled Russia to conduct reconnaissance and surveillance operations, as well as target Ukrainian military assets with precision strikes.

Ukraine, on the other hand, has also demonstrated its use of modern military technology, including drones and electronic warfare systems. Ukraine has made use of drones for reconnaissance and surveillance, as well as for targeting Russian military assets. Additionally, Ukraine has employed electronic warfare systems to disrupt Russian communication and navigation systems.

The conflict has also highlighted the importance of asymmetric warfare and unconventional tactics. Both sides have made use of irregular and paramilitary forces, as well as unconventional tactics such as cyber attacks and disinformation campaigns.

The use of hybrid warfare tactics, which combine conventional military tactics with non-military means such as economic pressure and propaganda, has also been a significant feature of the conflict. Russia has been accused of using such tactics in Ukraine, as well as in other conflicts such as the 2016 US presidential election.

The conflict has also highlighted the importance of intelligence gathering and analysis. The ability to gather and analyze information has been crucial in informing military decision-making and tactics on both sides of the conflict.

Overall, the conflict in Ukraine has showcased the use of modern military technology and strategies, as well as the importance of asymmetric warfare and unconventional tactics. The conflict has also highlighted the importance of intelligence gathering and analysis in modern warfare.

In addition to modern military technology and strategies, the conflict in Ukraine has also showcased the importance of international military cooperation and assistance.

Ukraine has received support from various international partners, including the United States, Canada, and the European Union. This support has included military aid, training, and advisory assistance.

NATO has also been involved in providing support to Ukraine. In 2014, NATO established a trust fund to support Ukrainian defense reform, and has provided training and advice to the Ukrainian military.

The conflict has also highlighted the importance of international arms control agreements, such as the Conventional Forces in Europe Treaty (CFE) and the Treaty on Open Skies. These agreements provide a framework for regulating and verifying military activities, and have been important in promoting transparency and trust between states.

However, the conflict in Ukraine has also led to concerns about the potential for a new arms race in Europe. The increased military spending and focus on military readiness by many countries in response to the crisis has led to concerns about a return to Cold War-era tensions.

The conflict has also highlighted the need for improved crisis management and conflict resolution mechanisms. The ongoing conflict in eastern Ukraine has been marked by a lack of progress in finding a lasting solution, and has led to continued suffering for civilians in the region.

In conclusion, the conflict in Ukraine has showcased the importance of modern military technology and strategies, as well as the need for international military cooperation and arms control agreements. However, it has also highlighted the potential for increased tensions and a new arms race in Europe, and the need for improved crisis management and conflict resolution mechanisms.

Chapter 15: Humanitarian Crisis and Civilian Suffering

The conflict in Ukraine has not only had a significant military impact, but it has also caused a severe humanitarian crisis and resulted in significant civilian suffering.

According to the United Nations, the conflict has resulted in over 13,000 deaths and 30,000 injuries, the majority of which are civilians. Additionally, over 1.5 million people have been internally displaced, while thousands of others have fled to neighboring countries.

The humanitarian crisis has been exacerbated by the ongoing fighting, which has disrupted access to basic services such as healthcare, education, and water and sanitation. The conflict has also damaged critical infrastructure such as power plants, which has led to prolonged electricity and heating shortages during the winter months.

The conflict has also resulted in significant economic hardship for many Ukrainians, particularly those living in the conflict-affected regions. The loss of jobs and disruption of economic activity has led to widespread poverty and food insecurity.

In addition to the direct impact on civilians, the conflict has also resulted in significant human rights abuses. Both sides have been accused of committing human rights violations, including extrajudicial killings, torture, and arbitrary detention.

Furthermore, the conflict has had a disproportionate impact on vulnerable groups such as women, children, and the elderly. Women and children are particularly vulnerable to sexual violence and exploitation, while the elderly face significant challenges accessing healthcare and basic services.

The humanitarian crisis in Ukraine has been further compounded by the COVID-19 pandemic. The pandemic has placed additional strain on an already overburdened healthcare system, while lockdown measures have worsened economic hardship for many Ukrainians.

In conclusion, the conflict in Ukraine has had a significant humanitarian impact, resulting in widespread civilian suffering and displacement, as well as human rights abuses. The ongoing humanitarian crisis has been further exacerbated by the COVID-19 pandemic, highlighting the urgent need for increased international humanitarian support and assistance.

Efforts to address the humanitarian crisis have been ongoing, with numerous international organizations providing aid and assistance to those affected by the conflict. However, access to those in need remains a challenge, particularly in areas controlled by separatist groups.

The United Nations and other humanitarian organizations have called for increased access to affected populations, particularly in areas where access has been restricted. In addition, there have been calls for the parties to the conflict to adhere to international humanitarian law and protect civilians from harm.

The conflict in Ukraine has also highlighted the need for greater attention to be paid to the protection of civilians in armed conflict. The International Committee of the Red Cross (ICRC) has called for greater efforts to be made to ensure that civilians are protected from harm, particularly in urban areas where the majority of civilian casualties occur.

In addition, the conflict has highlighted the importance of addressing the root causes of conflict and promoting long-term stability and peace. Addressing economic and political grievances, as well as promoting dialogue and reconciliation between conflicting parties, are critical to preventing future conflicts and minimizing the humanitarian impact of armed conflict.

Overall, the humanitarian crisis in Ukraine is a stark reminder of the devastating impact that armed conflict can have on civilian populations. It highlights the need for greater efforts to protect civilians in armed conflict, provide humanitarian assistance and support, and address the root causes of conflict to promote long-term stability and peace.

Chapter 16: Cyber Warfare

———

The conflict between Ukraine and Russia has not been limited to physical fighting and has also involved the use of cyber warfare. Cyber warfare refers to the use of computer technology to disrupt, damage, or gain unauthorized access to computer systems and networks.

The use of cyber warfare in the conflict has been particularly significant, with both sides using cyber attacks to gain a strategic advantage. These attacks have included the use of malware to disrupt critical infrastructure and the use of hacking techniques to gain access to sensitive information.

In 2015, Ukraine experienced a major cyber attack that targeted its power grid, resulting in a large-scale blackout. The attack was attributed to a Russian hacking group, and it highlighted the vulnerability of critical infrastructure to cyber attacks.

In addition to attacks on infrastructure, cyber warfare has also been used to spread disinformation and propaganda. Both sides have used social media and other online platforms to spread false information and influence public opinion.

The use of cyber warfare in the conflict has had a significant impact on both Ukraine and Russia. It has demonstrated the potential for cyber attacks to cause significant damage and disruption, and it has highlighted the need for improved cybersecurity measures to protect critical infrastructure.

In conclusion, the use of cyber warfare in the conflict between Ukraine and Russia has been significant and has demonstrated the potential for cyber attacks to cause significant damage and disruption. The use of cyber warfare highlights the need for improved cybersecurity measures and the importance of international cooperation in addressing this emerging threat.

As the conflict between Ukraine and Russia continues, the use of cyber warfare is likely to remain a key aspect of the conflict. Both sides will continue to develop and refine their cyber capabilities, and the use of cyber attacks to gain a strategic advantage will remain a key element of their overall strategies.

In response to the threat posed by cyber warfare, Ukraine has taken steps to improve its cybersecurity measures. In 2018, the country established a National Cybersecurity Coordination Center to coordinate its cybersecurity efforts and improve information sharing among government agencies.

International efforts to address the threat of cyber warfare have also increased in recent years. In 2019, NATO announced that it would recognize cyber attacks as a potential trigger for Article 5, which is the collective defense clause of the NATO treaty. This means that a significant cyber attack against a NATO member state could trigger a collective response from all member states.

The use of cyber warfare in the conflict between Ukraine and Russia highlights the importance of international cooperation in addressing this emerging threat. As the world becomes increasingly interconnected and reliant on technology, the potential for cyber attacks to cause significant damage and disruption will only increase. It is essential that countries work together to develop effective cybersecurity measures and strategies to prevent and respond to cyber attacks.

In conclusion, the use of cyber warfare in the conflict between Ukraine and Russia has highlighted the potential for cyber attacks to cause significant damage and disruption. It has also highlighted the need for improved cybersecurity measures and international cooperation to address this emerging threat. As the world becomes increasingly reliant on technology, the importance of effective cybersecurity measures and strategies will only continue to grow.

Chapter 17: International Response

The international community has been closely monitoring the Ukraine-Russia conflict since it began in 2014. The United Nations has played a significant role in the response to the conflict, calling for an immediate end to hostilities and a peaceful resolution to the crisis.

In March 2014, the UN General Assembly passed a resolution affirming Ukraine's territorial integrity and condemning Russia's annexation of Crimea. The UN has also established a mission to monitor the human rights situation in Ukraine and investigate alleged human rights violations.

In addition to the UN, other international organizations have also been involved in responding to the conflict. The European Union has imposed economic sanctions on Russia in response to its actions in Ukraine, while NATO has increased its presence in Eastern Europe to provide reassurance to its members in the region.

Individual countries have also taken action in response to the conflict. The United States and other Western nations have provided military aid to Ukraine to support its defense against Russian aggression. At the same time, Russia has received support from other countries, including China and Belarus.

Overall, the international response to the conflict has been mixed. While some countries and organizations have taken strong action to condemn Russian aggression and support Ukraine, others have been more hesitant to get involved. As the conflict continues, it remains to be seen what role the international community will play in bringing about a peaceful resolution to the crisis.

The international response to the Ukraine-Russia conflict has been a complex and evolving process, with many different countries and organizations involved in various ways. One of the key challenges in responding to the conflict has been the lack of consensus among the international community on the appropriate course of action.

The United Nations has played a critical role in responding to the conflict, both in terms of providing humanitarian assistance and advocating for a peaceful resolution to the crisis. However, the UN has faced significant challenges in its efforts to address the conflict, including a lack of cooperation from some parties involved and political obstacles at the Security Council.

The European Union has also been actively involved in the response to the conflict, imposing economic sanctions on Russia and providing financial and technical assistance to Ukraine. However, there have been divisions among EU member states over the appropriate response to the conflict, with some advocating for a more conciliatory approach towards Russia.

NATO has also played a significant role in responding to the conflict, with member countries increasing their military presence in Eastern Europe to provide reassurance to allies in the region. However, there have been concerns about the impact of this increased military activity on the stability of the region and the potential for escalation of the conflict.

In addition to international organizations, individual countries have also taken a range of actions in response to the conflict. The United States has been a key supporter of Ukraine, providing military aid and economic assistance to the country. Other countries, such as China and Belarus, have been more supportive of Russia in the conflict.

Chapter 18: Human Rights Violations

<hr>

The conflict between Ukraine and Russia has had significant human rights implications, particularly for those living in the conflict zone. Both sides have been accused of committing human rights violations, including torture, unlawful detention, and extrajudicial killings.

According to reports from the United Nations and other human rights organizations, the conflict has resulted in the displacement of over two million people, many of whom have been forced to flee their homes and seek refuge in other parts of Ukraine or abroad. These displaced persons face a range of challenges, including limited access to basic necessities such as food, water, and medical care.

There have also been numerous reports of violations of international humanitarian law, including attacks on civilian areas, the use of indiscriminate weapons, and the targeting of critical infrastructure such as hospitals and schools. These actions have had devastating consequences for civilians in the conflict zone, including a significant number of civilian casualties.

Both sides have been accused of committing human rights violations against members of the opposing side, including arbitrary detention and torture. Reports from the United Nations and other human rights organizations suggest that both

Ukrainian and Russian forces have engaged in these types of activities, and that they have been carried out with impunity.

In addition, there have been reports of human rights violations against minority groups, particularly the Crimean Tatars, who have faced harassment, discrimination, and persecution since the annexation of Crimea by Russia in 2014. Human rights organizations have documented cases of arbitrary detention, torture, and enforced disappearances of members of this group.

The international community has condemned these human rights violations and has called for those responsible to be held accountable. The United Nations, in particular, has established a monitoring mission in Ukraine to investigate human rights abuses and to provide assistance to victims.

Despite these efforts, the human rights situation in the conflict zone remains precarious, and there is an urgent need for greater protection of civilians and for those responsible for human rights violations to be brought to justice.

The conflict between Ukraine and Russia has been marked by widespread human rights violations, affecting both civilians and combatants. Reports of torture, abduction, and unlawful detention have been documented by international organizations such as Amnesty International, Human Rights Watch, and the United Nations Human Rights Office.

One of the most notable cases of human rights violations during the conflict is the annexation of Crimea by Russia in 2014. The annexation led to a deterioration of human rights in the region, with reports of arbitrary detentions, enforced disappearances, and torture of individuals who opposed the annexation. In addition, the Russian authorities have imposed restrictions on the rights to freedom of expression, assembly, and association, as well as targeting minority groups such as the Crimean Tatars.

In eastern Ukraine, both Ukrainian government forces and separatist groups have been accused of human rights abuses. The UN Human Rights Office reported that civilians have been subjected to enforced disappearances, torture, and extrajudicial killings. There have also been reports of the use of cluster munitions and other indiscriminate weapons in populated areas, leading to civilian casualties.

The conflict has also led to the displacement of millions of people, with many forced to flee their homes due to fighting or persecution. According to the UN Refugee Agency, as of 2021, there were over 1.4 million registered internally displaced persons in Ukraine and over 400,000 refugees and asylum seekers from Ukraine in neighboring countries.

The international community has condemned the human rights violations occurring in Ukraine and Russia, with various countries and organizations calling for an end to the conflict and the protection of civilians. The UN Human Rights Council has established a monitoring mission to document and report on human rights violations in Ukraine, and the International Criminal Court has opened an investigation into crimes committed during the conflict.

However, despite these efforts, human rights violations continue to occur, highlighting the urgent need for a peaceful resolution to the conflict that prioritizes the protection of human rights.

Chapter 19: Prospects for Peace

The ongoing conflict between Ukraine and Russia has caused immense suffering for both countries, including loss of life, displacement, and economic hardship. Despite the efforts of the international community to resolve the conflict, a lasting peace agreement has remained elusive. However, there are still reasons to remain hopeful for a peaceful resolution to the conflict.

One reason for optimism is the ongoing diplomatic efforts to find a solution to the conflict. The Minsk agreements, signed in 2015, were intended to provide a framework for ending the conflict through a ceasefire, the withdrawal of heavy weapons, and the establishment of a special status for certain areas of Donetsk and Luhansk. While the agreements have not yet been fully implemented, they represent a significant step towards a peaceful resolution of the conflict.

Another reason for hope is the role of civil society in promoting peace and reconciliation between Ukraine and Russia. Grassroots organizations, such as the Ukrainian Peacebuilding School and the Russian-Ukrainian Reconciliation Commission, have been working to build bridges between the two countries through dialogue and cultural exchange. These efforts can help to break down the barriers that have been created by the conflict and promote a shared understanding of the issues at stake.

However, there are also significant challenges to achieving peace in the region. The continued fighting and humanitarian crisis in eastern Ukraine, as well as Russia's annexation of Crimea, have created deep-seated mistrust between the two countries. The presence of Russian troops in Ukraine and the ongoing military buildup on the Russian side of the border also raise concerns about the possibility of further escalation.

In addition, the issue of Crimea remains a major obstacle to a peaceful resolution of the conflict. While Russia has refused to return the peninsula to Ukraine, the international community has largely rejected its annexation. The situation remains unresolved and tensions between Ukraine and Russia continue to simmer.

Despite these challenges, the prospects for peace in the region remain alive. Continued diplomatic efforts, grassroots initiatives, and a commitment to dialogue and reconciliation can help to lay the groundwork for a peaceful resolution of the conflict.

The conflict between Ukraine and Russia has resulted in the displacement of thousands of people, loss of life, and significant economic and social impacts on both countries. Despite diplomatic efforts to resolve the conflict, the situation remains tense, with occasional ceasefire violations and continued hostilities in the Donbass region.

The prospect for peace in the conflict remains uncertain. However, some steps have been taken towards a peaceful resolution. In 2015, the Minsk II agreement was signed by

Ukraine, Russia, France, and Germany, with the aim of resolving the conflict in the Donbass region. The agreement includes provisions for a ceasefire, the withdrawal of heavy weapons, and the implementation of constitutional reforms in Ukraine, including the granting of greater autonomy to the Donetsk and Luhansk regions.

Since the signing of the Minsk II agreement, there have been some efforts to implement its provisions. However, progress has been slow, and violations of the ceasefire continue to occur. In 2019, a new initiative known as the Normandy Format was launched, with the aim of restarting peace talks between Ukraine and Russia. The format includes representatives from Ukraine, Russia, Germany, and France, and aims to build on the Minsk II agreement to reach a lasting peace settlement.

Despite these diplomatic efforts, the situation on the ground remains tense, with ongoing hostilities and a lack of progress towards a lasting peace settlement. Many analysts believe that a comprehensive resolution to the conflict will require significant concessions from both sides, including the recognition of Ukraine's territorial integrity and the granting of greater autonomy to the Donbass region.

In addition to diplomatic efforts, civil society has also played an important role in promoting peace and reconciliation in the conflict. Non-governmental organizations, religious groups, and other grassroots organizations have organized peace rallies, interfaith dialogues, and other initiatives aimed at promoting dialogue and understanding between Ukrainians and Russians.

Ultimately, the prospects for peace in the conflict between Ukraine and Russia remain uncertain. However, ongoing diplomatic efforts and the role of civil society offer hope for a peaceful resolution to the conflict in the future.

Chapter 20: Conclusion

The conflict between Ukraine and Russia has had a profound impact on both countries and the wider international community. The conflict has been marked by military action, political maneuvering, and human rights violations, and has been shaped by geopolitical tensions and historic animosity.

Throughout the conflict, both Ukraine and Russia have been criticized for their actions. Ukraine has been accused of provoking the conflict by pursuing closer ties with the West and cracking down on pro-Russian separatists in the east, while Russia has been accused of illegally annexing Crimea and supporting separatist movements in eastern Ukraine.

The international community has responded to the conflict in a variety of ways, with some countries imposing economic sanctions on Russia and others offering diplomatic support to Ukraine. The United Nations has played a role in trying to mediate the conflict, although progress has been slow.

Despite the ongoing conflict, there are still prospects for peace. Diplomatic efforts continue, and civil society groups are working to promote dialogue and reconciliation. However, any lasting peace will require a willingness on both sides to compromise and address the underlying issues driving the conflict.

In conclusion, the Ukraine-Russia conflict is a complex and ongoing conflict with far-reaching implications for both countries and the international community as a whole. The conflict has had a profound impact on the lives of individuals in Ukraine and Russia, as well as on the geopolitical landscape of the region.

Despite ongoing diplomatic efforts and the involvement of international organizations such as the UN, the conflict shows little sign of a peaceful resolution in the immediate future. The conflict has also raised important questions about the nature of modern warfare, the role of technology and propaganda, and the importance of human rights in times of conflict.

Moving forward, it will be important for both Ukraine and Russia to continue engaging in diplomatic efforts aimed at achieving a lasting peace. It will also be important for the international community to continue supporting these efforts and holding both sides accountable for any human rights violations or other unlawful acts committed during the conflict.

Ultimately, the resolution of the Ukraine-Russia conflict will require a combination of political will, international support, and a commitment to finding a peaceful and just solution that respects the rights and dignity of all individuals involved.

Looking forward, the conflict remains unresolved, and tensions continue to simmer. Despite diplomatic efforts to find a solution, the situation on the ground remains volatile, and there is a risk of further escalation. The conflict has already had a significant human toll, and there are concerns that it could continue to claim lives and destabilize the region.

In conclusion, the Ukraine-Russia conflict is a complex and multifaceted conflict that has had significant regional and global implications. Its roots lie in historical, political, and economic factors, and it has been characterized by a range of military and non-military tactics, including cyber warfare, propaganda, and economic sanctions. The conflict has had a profound impact on the people of Ukraine and Russia and has strained relations between Russia and the West. Despite ongoing diplomatic efforts, the situation remains unresolved, and there is a risk of further escalation.

As of April 2023 the war is still ongoing with no clear ending in sight.